AQUARIUS

# AQUARIUS

## January 20–February 18

# Crystal Astrology for Modern Life

SANDY SITRON

# CONTENTS

# AQUARIUS THROUGHOUT THE YEAR

# LUNAR ENERGY AND MERCURY IN MOTION

# CRYSTALS, ASTROLOGY AND YOU

# THE STONES, THE SIGNS AND YOU

The stars above you and the stones beneath your feet are part of the fabric of your world. Astrology offers a cosmic perspective. Crystals radiate with the healing energy of the Earth. Together, they serve as guides in your life, engaged in a vibrational conversation that can help you reflect on, and tune into, who you are. Birthstones and other crystals can be used to highlight and harness the energy of your astrological birth chart.

As above, so below – harness the power of crystals and the cosmos to create a deeper connection with yourself for a confident, empowered, high-vibe life.

Astrology is the ancient study of the changing positions and alternating energy of the celestial bodies and how this relates to our lives on Earth. The unique cosmic environment that you synced up with at the moment of your first breath provides awareness of – and offers a way to interpret – your personality traits, core strengths, growth areas, emotional style and so much more. When you better understand your vibrational self, it's easier to make informed choices about the big and small things in your life. Your conscious perspective is uplifted. Your mind is opened and activated.

Crystals, or 'stones', vibrate with the breath of the Earth. They act on an energetic level, sending vibrations out into the world. They are natural amplifiers of positive energy and bring discordant energies into balance. Each crystal has its own energy blueprint, which is why different types of stones may influence the human energy field in different ways. Pairing the insight that you gain from astrology with the healing power of crystals can help you navigate certain life areas and facilitate personal transformation and spiritual growth throughout the astrological year.

Crystals and the constellations call to us. In this book you'll receive a bespoke selection of crystals to help you amplify or balance the unique energies of your sign. You'll gain insight into your life, activate your highest potential and learn to live harmoniously with the energy that surrounds you.

When gazing at the night sky, when you hold a crystal in your hand, feel inspired to slow down, be present in the moment and get ready to embark on a meaningful journey of self-discovery.

## YOUR UNIQUE RECOMMENDATIONS

We all accept that different things work for different people. Advice that's a perfect fit for one person might fall flat for someone else. Regardless of where Aquarius sits in your personal astrology, this book will help you understand your Aquarius nature and give you specific crystal recommendations for your sign and each astrological season. You can use these bespoke Aquarius crystals to build confidence, spark creativity, feel more present, harmonize relationships, attract love, embrace your emotions, cultivate friendships, create abundance, optimize your health and wellness, amplify your natural gifts and find balance.

## YOUR ASTRO-CRYSTAL JOURNEY

Once you understand how the two energetic studies of crystals and astrology relate to your life, you'll be ready to take a deep dive into your Aquarius energy and learn to use crystals to leverage the strengths of your Aquarius gifts, whether Aquarius is your Sun, Moon or Rising sign, or elsewhere in your unique astrology. You'll also discover your unique Aquarius crystal recommendations for love, friendship, money, work and health to help you connect to your true potential and reach your dreams and goals.

As each astrological season holds a different kind of energy, this book will take you through the year and show you how crystals can help you channel your unique Aquarius energy under each sign. In this way, you will learn to navigate through the seasons with ease and to harmonize with the cycles of nature. You will discover how crystals can help you embrace the ebb and flow of the 29-day Moon cycle, enable you to sail through Mercury Retrograde and even plan your week.

This book is part of a series that unites each of the twelve zodiac signs with recommended crystals. When you are ready to go deeper on your astro-crystal journey, you may choose to purchase the companion books in the series that correspond to the other prominent signs in your birth chart.

# THE
# STONES

Dazzling gemstones are typically formed deep under the Earth's surface, stimulated by the combination of mineral-rich water, heat and pressure. Subterranean 'gardens' nurture the formation of billions of atoms into highly ordered, three-dimensional repeating patterns to create unique crystals, each one holding a vibrational record of earthly, physical reality.

Across the world and over millennia, people have been fascinated by crystals. Lucent jewels have captured the imagination for over 30,000 years. In the Democratic Republic of the Congo, small tools decorated with Quartz have been found that date back to 33,000 BCE. The Ancient Sumerians of Mesopotamia (present-day Iraq) used crystals for rituals and magic in the fourth century BCE. Humankind has used crystals for decoration, status, currency, religion, healing, magic-making and, in more recent times, modern technology. Early radios used crystals as electrical and tuning components. Today's computers, LCD screens and some batteries rely on crystal technology.

**Good Vibrations**   People across different cultures and generations have turned to crystals as guides or helpers because it seems that, whatever facet of earthly experience you are struggling with, there is a crystal frequency that can help you move forwards on your path. Crystals may help bring calm and heal stress, empower you when you need support or confidence, or provide focus and clarity when you're struggling with an important decision. Crystals are thought to absorb the energy that you are trying to release and release the energy you are trying to absorb.

For example, if you are feeling dull and listless, Carnelian may share with you a vibration of high energy and drive. If you are overheated or stressed, Rose Quartz may help you soften and relax. Choosing the right crystal that resonates with, or reacts to, your energy can shift your mood or your mindset.

# CHOOSING YOUR CRYSTALS

In Part Two of this book, you will be guided to a selection of crystals that are energetically aligned with your unique astrology. If you are adding these stones to your collection, it's important to choose responsibly.

**Sustainability and Ethics**   How did the crystal that you have in your hand make its way to you? The answer to this question is incredibly important to the well-being of humanity and the Earth.

The crystal industry is shrouded in mystery and plagued by bad practices. When you purchase a crystal, make sure to find gems that have a traceable, and short, journey from the mine to your hand. It's important to know if the mine that the crystal came from uses ethical, safe and sustainable practices. Discover if the lapidary, where the crystal was cut and polished, is a safe place that pays a living wage to the people who work there. The easiest way to do this is to mindfully source your crystals from sellers who have done the legwork. You vote with your financial choices. Make sure that you are contributing to better health and safety for all.

More information about sustainable and ethical practices and purveyors can be found on my website www.sandysitron.com/crystals.

**Size, Finish and Price**   When harnessing the power of a crystal for personal use, the size of the stone doesn't matter. If you are holding a crystal or carrying it close to your body, its vibration is in your energy field and will have an effect whatever its size.

A raw stone is a stone that is untreated. These are just as effective to use in healing practices as a crystal that has been tumbled or polished. So when you are choosing a crystal, choose one that appeals to you, no matter the size or finish.

The stones selected in this book can be sourced at an affordable price. Although some of the stones mentioned may sound ultra-luxurious and expensive, these crystals are available at a range of values.

# YOUR CRYSTAL TOOLKIT

In the next section, you'll find crystal recommendations for your specific sign. First, here are a few indispensable crystals to round out your toolkit. These selections are a wonderful support for anyone at any time.

**Smoky Quartz**   Getting grounded is the basis of spiritual work. So many factors in everyday life pull us out of ourselves. Spending too much time on your phone, not enough time in nature or eating too much sugar are common culprits, but the list goes on. If you want to nail your next meeting at work, remember where your keys are, or get on top of that to-do list, you need to get grounded. Feeling grounded also allows you to be present in your relationships and tuned in to your physical needs. This is where Smoky Quartz can help. This crystal keeps you centred, and emotionally clear. It may help you take a more practical view of a situation. On a more mystical level, Smoky Quartz has the effect of protecting you from energetic drains on your system. It is an excellent protection stone and just holding it can help you feel steady.

**Selenite**   Just as you bathe your body regularly, it makes sense to regularly cleanse your energy system too. Energetic cleansing can help you balance your emotions and clear your mind. Cleanse your energy after work, socializing or spending time in a crowd. Or employ Selenite to help you get rid of emotional residue after a tough conversation. Energy cleansing is also recommended when you are going through any kind of transition – a break-up, a move or some other important milestone. Use Selenite with the intention of purifying your energy field and cleansing yourself of anything that is dragging you down. Imagine that it shines a ray of light through your entire body, clearing and cleansing.

| Smoky Quartz Ritual | Selenite Ritual |
|---|---|
| Perform the grounding practice on page 26 while holding Smoky Quartz to anchor you. | Selenite can also be used to cleanse the energy of your other stones. Place a Selenite stone next to your crystals overnight. |

## SOOTHING
## RELAXATION

**Rose Quartz**  We all know what it's like to get stressed out and frazzled. Sometimes the nervous system is overloaded and it's hard to calm down. When that happens, you need a soothing crystal ally that can help you relax. If you are having trouble sleeping, are feeling on edge, or are working through some challenging emotions, it's time to soften with Rose Quartz. This dreamy pink stone is known for its inherent ability to calm and reassure. It soothes you while strengthening your capacity for empathy and compassion. If you're feeling down, lonely or heartbroken, let this crystalline stress-reliever support you.

## FINDING
## YOUR DIRECTION

**Clear Quartz**  Clear quartz is a true all-purpose stone. When you actively set an intention with Clear Quartz, the stone will magnify that intention. When your world is changing around you and you need to forge ahead in a new direction, Clear Quartz will get you there. Clear Quartz can help you clarify, strategize and set your aspirations for your life. Once programmed with your wishes and desires, this powerful amplifier will hold the vibration of your intentions and help you visualize and realize your future.

| Rose Quartz Ritual | Clear Quartz Ritual |
| --- | --- |
| Infuse a tumbled Rose Quartz stone in your next cup of tea or glass of water for a mindful moment with a soothing elixir. | Write an affirmation that inspires you. Say your affirmation aloud while holding Clear Quartz. |

**Amethyst**   Your intuition is your natural guidance system. It's that gut feeling you have when something feels wrong, or when something feels just right. Intuition shows up in different ways for everyone but it's like a muscle that can be strengthened. If you have questions about your life and you want to tune into the answers, Amethyst is at your service. In those moments, practice asking and listening and let this violet stone help open up your mind's eye. Amethyst is also a fantastic friend when you need help saying the right thing in your next important conversation, meeting or presentation. Or if you are looking for a sparkling boost to your creativity, open the channels of inspiration with Amethyst by your side.

|  | Amethyst Ritual |  |
| --- | --- | --- |

The next time you have a question about your life or
path, lie down and place an Amethyst stone on your forehead or
near the crown of your head. Meditate and make space for
the answer to come through.

# THE SIGNS

## ASTROLOGY AND YOU

You are a unique being, made up of a solar system of characteristics that define your identity. Astrology illuminates your personality and your path. It describes how you think, learn, love, act and much more. Astrology can also be used to understand the energy of the moment.

Astrology has been contributed to by cultures throughout the world over thousands of years. The astrology used in this book is drawn from contemporary Western astrology. Like all things in the universe, the movements of the planets through the zodiac create a vibration. At the moment of your first breath, this energy is mirrored within you.

Your astrology is much more complex than just your star sign. The movements of the planets under the zodiac, in the exact place, at the exact moment you were born form your birth chart, a personalized map of the sky from your unique vantage point on Earth when you took your first breath. As well as showing you where the Sun lands in your chart, denoting your star sign, it also shows under which signs the Moon and other planets fall – this is the key to understanding your personal energetic code.

In order to discover your unique astrological make-up first you need to map your birth chart.

## SUN, MOON AND RISING SIGN

When someone asks, 'What's your sign?' they are actually referring to your Sun sign, but it's worth learning your Moon and Rising signs too. These three symbols are a good place to begin your astrological journey as they represent the basic outline of who you are – like a simple sketch that captures your likeness in just a few brushstrokes. Together these three symbols make up your inner and outer self.

**Casting Your Birth Chart**   Go to www.sandysitron.com/crystals and enter your birth data in the 'Create Your Birth Chart' tool. You'll then receive your birth chart, also called your natal chart, that shows the signs that the planets were in when you were born, and where they were located in the sky.

## SUN
## SIGN

· The Sun is a constant bright light, it symbolizes your ego, the part of you that you consciously identify with. It's how you tend to think of yourself.

· The Sun is the gravitational centre of the solar system, it represents your core self and describes your fundamental character and values.

· The Sun is the energy source that creates life on our planet, it signifies how you channel your energy.

## MOON
## SIGN

· The Moon is most visible at night, it symbolizes the part of you that is hard to see – your subconscious self.

The Moon changes shape through the lunar month. It represents your ever-changing emotions and how you respond subconsciously to your feelings.

The Moon is a satellite that circles the Earth, it describes how you turn inwards to protect, nurture and soothe yourself.

## RISING
## SIGN

· The Rising sign, also known as your Ascendant, is the constellation of the zodiac that was rising on the eastern horizon at the precise moment of your birth.

· The Rising sign shines new light into the world. It symbolizes how the rays of your personality beam out ahead as you walk down the street, meet new people, or interact on social media. It represents your vibe or your 'brand'. It epitomizes how other people see you.

· As you explore the following pages, you'll learn how to balance and enhance your unique energy using supportive crystals. This book will also help you find alignment and teach you how to leverage your inherent gifts.

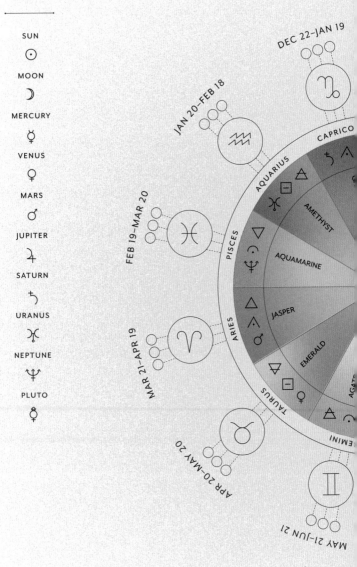

## PLANETS

SUN ☉

MOON ☽

MERCURY ☿

VENUS ♀

MARS ♂

JUPITER ♃

SATURN ♄

URANUS ⛢

NEPTUNE ♆

PLUTO ♇

DEC 22–JAN 19 ♑

JAN 20–FEB 18 ♒

FEB 19–MAR 20 ♓

MAR 21–APR 19 ♈

APR 20–MAY 20 ♉

MAY 21–JUN 21 ♊

CAPRICORN

AQUARIUS

AMETHYST

PISCES

AQUAMARINE

ARIES

JASPER

TAURUS

EMERALD

AGATE

GEMINI

DATES ARE APPROXIMATE AS THE DATES OF THE
SIGNS VARY BY ABOUT A DAY FROM YEAR TO YEAR.

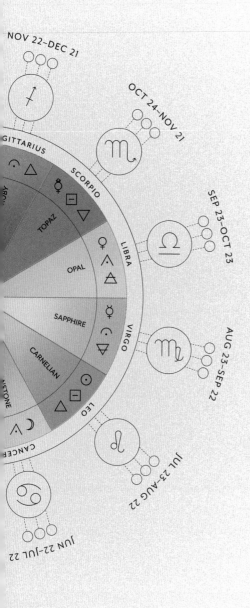

FIRE

△

EARTH

▽

AIR

△

WATER

▽

NOV 22–DEC 21

OCT 24–NOV 21

SEP 23–OCT 23

AUG 23–SEP 22

JUL 23–AUG 22

JUN 22–JUL 22

SAGITTARIUS

SCORPIO

TOPAZ

LIBRA

OPAL

VIRGO

SAPPHIRE

CARNELIAN

LEO

CANCER

MOONSTONE

MODALITY

CARDINAL

△

FIXED

□

MUTABLE

⌒

# TOOLS FOR
# YOUR JOURNEY

As you go forwards on your astro-crystal journey,
two key tools can help you gain insight and create positive
change – intuition and intention. Intuition helps you know
what you want and intention helps you make it happen.

## LETTING YOUR
## INTUITION GUIDE YOU

Everyone is intuitive, your intuition or 'inner knowing' is your built-in guidance system. Use the following prompts to strengthen your inner voice.

### How to Connect
### with Your Intuition

**Slow down**   Take a few deep breaths and close your eyes. The more you can slow down in your life (even for just five minutes) the louder your intuitive voice grows.

**Pose a question**   What do you want to know? Ask yourself. Say it aloud or ponder it silently. Or choose to write it down, sketch it or even dance it out. However you pose the question, make sure it is clear. If you aren't sure what to ask, try, 'what do I need to know that I don't yet know?'

**Listen for the answer**   You might hear words or notice a sensation in your body. You might write down your question in a notebook then flip the page and write down the answer. You might have an emotional response or feel compelled to move in a certain way. Pay attention.

**Practice**   The more you practice asking and listening, the more you get to understand your unique intuitive voice. Just as weightlifting tones your physical body, practicing these steps improves your intuitive muscle, so stick with it!

## INTENTION SETTING

In your meditations and rituals, you can program
your crystals with the intentions or affirmations
that will help you meet your goals.
An intention is a new thought that you would
like to think. Our subconscious minds save
energy by putting certain thoughts and habits on
repeat. This survival skill has benefits, such as
giving us more energy and space for other things,
but it also has its downsides, such as getting us
stuck in a negative pattern. One way to break in
a new way of thinking is to intentionally repeat
a new thought. Here is how to 'affirm' your new
way of thinking into being!

Define what it is you would like to change. Where are you feeling stuck? What is the pattern that is bugging you? For example, 'I am stuck because I have these exciting ideas for new projects, but I never finish what I start.'

- <u>Decide what you want</u>
  For instance, 'It would be great if I finished my projects.'

- <u>Make it an 'I' statement</u>
  Such as, 'I finish my projects.'

- <u>Make it affirmative</u>
  Make sure your affirmation is positively stated. Say what you want, not what you don't want. So 'I finish my projects' not 'I no longer leave my projects unfinished'.

- <u>Make it in the here and now</u>
  Write your affirmation in the present tense: 'I finish my projects' rather than 'I will finish my projects'.

- <u>Describe the feeling</u>
  Include some descriptors, so that you can easily visualize how great it feels to realize your affirmation: 'I finish my projects and I feel so satisfied.'

- <u>Evaluate</u> Does the affirmation you wrote give you a positive feeling? If so, wonderful! You have your affirmation. If not, refine it. You may need a 'stepping stone' to make your affirmation more believable. For example, if you have a complicated track record with finishing what you begin, your subconscious mind may need more help believing 'I finish my projects and I feel so satisfied'. In that case try, 'I believe in the possibility that I finish my projects and feel satisfied', or 'I'm learning to finish my projects with satisfaction and ease'. With time and practice you'll find that you no longer need the stepping stone and you can update your affirmation to 'I easily finish my projects and I'm filled with satisfaction!'

# WAYS TO
# WORK WITH
# CRYSTALS

Crystals are a powerful force as they are but,
in order to optimize their benefits, discover how
to care for and recharge them with regular
cleansing, and learn how to activate them using
the intentions you've developed.

# CLEANSE YOUR CRYSTALS

Everything on Earth must go through a process of decay and renewal. Cleansing your crystals can help them reset with a clear energetic frequency. When you cleanse a crystal, imagine that you are clearing it of any energy that it may have picked up from yourself, other people and the environment.

## How to Cleanse Your Crystals

Make sure to research your stone to discover if the method you are considering is safe for both you and the crystal. For example, some crystals may dissolve in water or fade in sunlight. Some stones contain trace minerals that may be physically harmful when released into water.

**Light:** Place your crystal in sunlight or moonlight for an hour.
**Salt:** Immerse your crystal in salt for about five minutes.
**Sound:** Chant or use an instrument such as singing bowls, chimes or tuning forks.
**Water:** Wash your crystal under running water, from a natural water source or a tap, for a few minutes.
**Visualization:** Imagine crystalline light or archangels surrounding your crystal with the intention of cleansing.
**Selenite:** Place selenite next to your crystal and leave in place overnight.
**Earth:** Bury your crystal underground for about a day.

### When to cleanse your crystals

It's a good idea to cleanse your crystal when you first get it and about once a month after that. Cleanse more often if you use your crystals regularly.

## GROUND
## YOURSELF

Before you do any kind of energy work, it's important to get grounded. When a ship puts down its anchor in a quiet harbour, it's protected from being pulled by strong waves back into the sea. As you engage in energy work with crystals, you may drift and dream far afield. It protects you to have an anchor that keeps you connected to the Earth.

### How to Get Grounded

- To begin, set yourself up in a quiet and comfortable space, either seated or lying down. Close your eyes. Imagine that your torso is like a tree trunk with roots growing down through your feet.

- Breathe comfortably and deeply as you imagine your roots flowing down through the ground and all the way to the Earth's core.

- Visualize a healing light moving up through your roots into your body. Imagine this healing light circulating through your body and carrying any tension or stress away and out, and back down into the Earth.

- Continue to imagine the energy flow – grounding energy coming up through your roots, tension and stress flowing back down to the Earth.

- When you feel relaxed and grounded, give thanks to the Earth before you open your eyes.

## ACTIVATE YOUR
## CRYSTALS

Now that your crystal is cleansed and you are grounded, you can 'program' your crystal with the intention you've developed. Programming your crystal is one way to activate it so that its vibrations are attuned to your desires and goals. It's as simple as telling your crystal what you intend to create or achieve.

### How to Program
### Your Intention

To amplify your crystal's power, focus your thoughts on your intention and train that energy towards your crystal.

- Make sure you have a clear intention or affirmation.

- Set a timer for ten minutes.

- Sit comfortably either in a chair or on the floor.

- Hold your crystal or place it on your body. You could also place it on the floor or on a table in front of you.

- On each inhale, repeat your intention out loud or in your mind.

- On each exhale bring your attention to your crystal.

- When you notice your attention wandering, bring your awareness back to the crystal and your breath.

- Repeat until your timer sounds.

# AQUARIUS

DATES: JANUARY 20–FEBRUARY 18 ELEMENT: AIR
MODALITY: FIXED PLANET: URANUS SYMBOL: WATER-BEARER
CRYSTAL: AMETHYST

# YOUR SIGN, EXPLAINED

Intelligent, innovative, humanitarian Aquarius. This is the sign that is ready to change the world. As an Aquarius, you think big, and you think outside the box. You have the ability to conceptualize a better way of life, not just for yourself but for everyone. The well-being of the greater community is important to you. You know that teamwork makes the dream work, and we only succeed if everyone thrives together in a healthy environment.

Your insight is razor sharp but you may take this special brand of genius for granted. You're constantly flooded with great ideas, so choosing which ones to invest in becomes important. Although you have a strong penchant for innovation and change, once you become deeply inspired by a concept or idea you tend to follow through. You are resilient and determined. When you become devoted to a cause, person, project or belief, nothing stands in your way.

Aquarius is the sign that rules the future. On a personal level, this can manifest in many ways. Maybe you are a trendsetter, or you have a keen sense of the next wave of ideas, fashions, technologies and innovation. You may find that you can easily visualize or imagine goals for your personal future or your community's collective future. With your ability to think ten steps ahead, you offer society a fresh perspective.

You are like an electrical current, you illuminate your surroundings, and you power through with consistency.

## AQUARIUS IS AN
## AIR SIGN

Air flows through and around every creature on Earth. It is invisible but touches everything. In astrology, the Air element symbolizes mental and social connections. You offer conversation and curiosity, ready to discover what connects us all.

## AQUARIUS IS A
## TRANSPERSONAL SIGN

Transpersonal signs extend beyond the personal to live and work for the benefit of all people. These signs tend to consider the big picture and can factor other people's feelings and experiences into their beliefs, goals and dreams.

## AQUARIUS IS A
## FIXED SIGN

The fixed signs dig in and hold on. This energy keeps projects going, even when times are tough. Aquarius's lasting energy helps you meet your long-term goals. Slow and steady wins the race.

## AQUARIUS IS RULED BY
## THE PLANET URANUS

Uranus symbolizes innovations, new ideas and non-conformist attitudes. This ruling planet imbues Aquarius with the ability to shake up the status quo and open minds to new ideas.

## THE WATER-BEARER IS THE
## SYMBOL FOR AQUARIUS

This humanitarian symbol represents a person who brings life (water) to others.

## AMETHYST IS A KEY CRYSTAL
## BIRTHSTONE FOR AQUARIUS

This vibrant purple crystal is soothing and serene. It protects the mind and spirit so that Aquarians can think clearly, focus on brilliant ideas and take the moral high road in conversation. You enjoy feeling connected with society but interacting with large groups of people can be draining for anyone. Amethyst's shielding qualities help you feel steady as you mix and mingle.

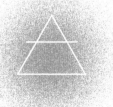

# AQUARIUS
## TRAITS

---

Your key traits show how you shine.
These are the special characteristics
that make you unique.

---

**Innovative**   You have the spirit of
an inventor. When faced with a
problem, your analytical mind scans
for creative solutions.

**Intelligent**   One might even say that
you have a genius streak. Your mind
is sharp.

**Social**   You're good with people. Others
feel comfortable around you. Sometimes
you feel like an outsider, but no-one else
thinks of you that way. You're an integral
part of your vast community.

**Objective**   Your natural ability to
be objective helps you keep calm in
most situations. Usually, you don't take
things personally.

**Conceptual**   You have a knack for
understanding abstract concepts.

**Unique**   You naturally express your
individuality, and you aren't afraid to be
a bit non-conformist. You aren't swayed
by what other people think. Some may
call you eclectic, or even eccentric, but
when it comes down to it, you are just
being yourself.

**Humanitarian**   That big heart of
yours gets fired up when you consider
injustice in the world. You care deeply
about human welfare.

**Visionary**   You can easily imagine the
future and you're always thinking a few
steps ahead.

# AQUARIUS GIFTS
## AND GROWTH AREAS

Your natural gifts offer both strengths and
challenges. The same traits that make you
special may also require balance at times.

### Freethinking vs Fighting
A freethinker, you go your own way.
It's fine to be non-conformist, but
at times you might fight needlessly
against tradition. You can be
instinctively disruptive.

### Unbiased vs Uninvolved
Your penchant for objectivity helps you
not take things personally. However,
when your talent for neutrality skews
towards detachment, you might start to
feel disconnected from others.

### Dynamic vs Erratic
You can be
charismatic and lively. Unafraid of
change, you certainly keep things
interesting! When your electric energy
reaches extremes, you might seem a
bit erratic.

### Imaginative vs Inattentive
Imaginative and creative, your mind is
always racing ten steps ahead, so you
may find it hard to focus on the details
of the present moment. You might not
remember where you put your keys, but
who cares when you are busy tackling
climate change and other world issues!

### Self-assured vs Stubborn
You know
what you think, and you know what you
want. When you are set on an idea, you
might dig your heels in.

### Cool vs Hot-tempered
At a young
age, you may have learned to downplay
your emotions so, as an adult, you can
be cool and controlled. But you may
find that habitually holding back your
feelings can lead to moody explosions.

Compatibility is a complex feature of astrology because you are more than just your Sun sign. And other people are multi-faceted too.

### Friends

**Aries** and Aquarius are equally visionary. As a dynamic pair, you'll either be making fashion statements, founding innovative start-ups or sparking revolutions.

You just can't stop talking when **Gemini** is around. The Gemini–Aquarius combo inspires hilarious jokes, genius brainstorming sessions and witty banter.

You're on the same page as **Libra**. You share a penchant for objectivity and clarity. At times, it seems as if the two of you might be able to solve the world's problems.

When it comes to drafting dreams and visions for the future, **Sagittarius** helps you believe that anything is possible.

### Foes

**Cancer's** emotional waterworks may dampen your spirits.

You have a handle on the big picture, and **Virgo** is an expert at the details. While there are moments when this combo works, usually you feel inconvenienced by the unnecessary fuss.

**Capricorn** is inspired by tradition, while you're more interested in innovation.

**Pisces** is subjective and emotional, while Aquarius is objective and analytical. It's hard to meet in the middle.

| | | | |
|---|---|---|---|
| ♈ | ♎ | ♋ | ♑ |
| ARIES | LIBRA | CANCER | CAPRICORN |
| ♊ | ♐ | ♍ | ♓ |
| GEMINI | SAGITTARIUS | VIRGO | PISCES |

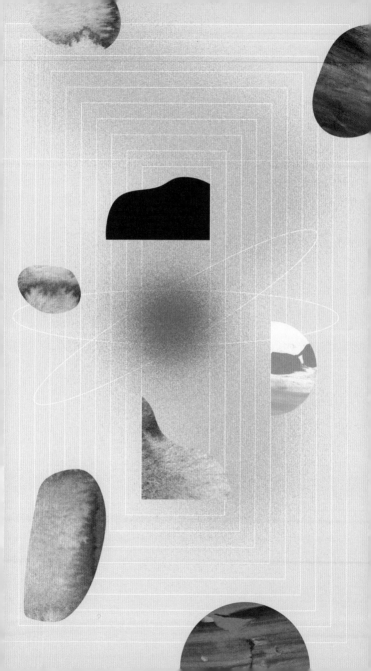

# AQUARIUS
# SUN

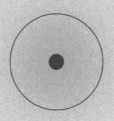

If you were born January 20–February 18, Aquarius is your Sun sign (check your birth chart for an exact calculation). Your Sun sign describes your basic energy.

Just as the Sun is the centre of the solar system, your Sun sign (also called your zodiac sign or star sign) symbolizes the core of your being. As an Aquarius Sun, you deeply value innovation, progress and collaboration. You are ready to get involved in your community and build a better world. Goals, visions and dreams for the future fuel you.

At times you may need to remind yourself that you are loved and included. And you may need to work on how you process your feelings so that you feel tuned in to your emotional experience.

Because your Sun sign fuels your confidence and enlivens your sense of self, there are two recommended crystals for Aquarius Sun. The Amplifying crystal will help you expand upon your gifts and the Balancing crystal will help you integrate your growth areas.

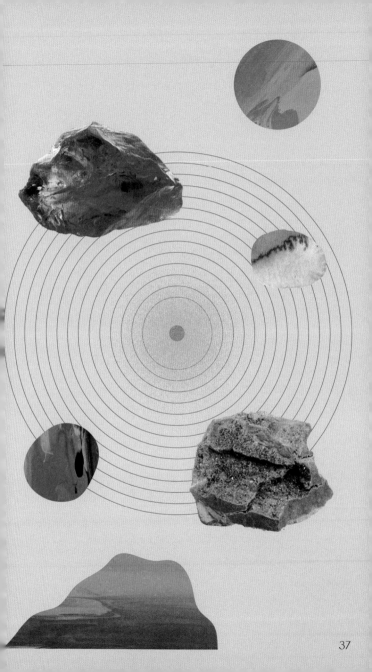

# AQUARIUS SUN AMPLIFYING CRYSTAL

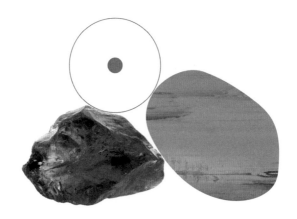

### CLARITY, WISDOM, SERENITY

**Amethyst** When you need to ramp up your brain power, reach for this gentle stone to encourage your best ideas and decisions. You are already a great thinker – let Amethyst act like your clarifying mental tonic. This plum-coloured crystal in the silicate family helps you clear your mind and inspires your scintillating brilliance.

Amethyst helps you share these brilliant thoughts with other people, by softening your communication skills so that you speak diplomatically and with wisdom. It helps you tune into your higher mind, so that you conduct yourself honestly, ethically and with grace.

You love to mingle in public and socialize. Amethyst offers a protective vibration that can help you feel shielded from everyone else's energy, opinions and emotions. This crystal is wonderfully calming, and it can help steady you in chaotic moments.

# AQUARIUS SUN
# BALANCING CRYSTAL

## WARMTH, CONNECTION,
## SUNNY DISPOSITION

**Amber**  Like a hot-water bottle for your soul, Amber helps you feel like you are glowing. Amber is not a mineral but a fossilized natural botanical resin. Once part of a living, breathing tree, Amber reminds you to live life to the fullest and to stay connected with your community.

This spoonful of sunshine warms your heart. Aquarians can sometimes feel isolated or left out, so let this enthusiastic crystal convince you that you're not alone and that your unique qualities are appreciated. In this way, Amber can help you hold a positive and joyful perspective on your life.

Amber can also help you work with your emotions. This golden resin is a general stress-reliever. It raises your spirits, and helps your feelings flow like the sap of a tree. With this uplifting support, you may find it easier to make space for your feelings and compassionately validate your emotional experience.

# AQUARIUS MOON

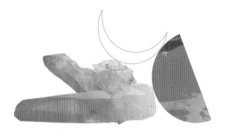

## ENERGY, CREATIVITY, TRANSFORMATION

In the same way that the Moon always appears to be changing shape in the sky, the Moon in your chart symbolizes the part of you that is always changing – your emotions.

Imagine that when you have an emotion come up, the Aquarius part of you steps to centre stage. This happens throughout the day. It doesn't matter if the emotion is happiness, sadness, frustration or exhilaration – when emotions arise you go into full Aquarius mode. Your erratic, playful, intellectual, independent, detached, moody and eccentric side is accentuated.

As an Aquarius Moon, you love to change things up and test out new endeavours. Progress soothes your spirits. Your emotions are often activated when you ponder your future, your goals and your dreams. You can get even more worked up about topics that pertain to the greater community. For example, you are a fierce advocate for freedom, justice and other humanitarian values.

When you were young, you may have found it easier to ignore your feelings or talk yourself out of processing

them. If that was the case, you may feel detached from your emotional process, and at times overwhelmed by waves of strong feelings that seem to rise up out of nowhere and then pass just as quickly. To work with this tendency, try to sit with your feelings as they arise.

**Tangerine Quartz**  Like its namesake fruit, this, pale orange crystal offers a zesty burst of energy. It stimulates your creativity, helping you find unique solutions. This process always puts you in a good mood. Thinking about 'what's possible' spurs you forwards and keeps you in high spirits.

This little spot of sunshine also helps you accept and work with transformation. And, since you are constantly sparking new breakthroughs, a positive view of change (especially the unexpected variety) does you wonders.

It's vital that you take the time to process your feelings as they arise. Tangerine Quartz helps you work with your emotions in a practical way. It offers a sense of gentle stability so that you feel supported.

# AQUARIUS RISING

### HARMONY, ACCEPTANCE,
### COMMUNICATION

Your Rising Sign is the sign that was on the eastern horizon when you were born. It represents the face you show to the world – your social personality. As an Aquarius Rising, your unique qualities sparkle and shimmer. You are singular. Depending on the day, you give off a first impression of being either friendly or a loner. You're not afraid to contradict yourself, as you can be both responsible and scatterbrained, detached and emotional, adaptable and resolute. In more ways than one, your personality is an enigma.

Other people perceive you to be eccentric, intelligent and idealistic. When it comes to group endeavours, your ability to think conceptually often wins you a leadership role. Your creativity is unmatched and other people take cues from you when it comes to trends and fashions. It's as though you are tuned into the collective consciousness and can sense the next 'in' thing.

As an Aquarius Rising, you are supported by a crystal that helps you communicate with clarity while feeling accepted by yourself and others.

**Angelite**   This sky-blue stone has an uplifting, soprano vibration. True to its celestial name, Angelite offers a feather-soft touch and a promise of experiencing heaven on Earth.

Aquarius Rising yearns for acceptance. This gentle crystal imparts a harmony that helps you trust that you are included and cared for. Let love in, and feel connected, supported and honoured by those around you.

Angelite supports crystal-clear communication. Reach for this crystal when you need to make yourself understood. Angelite can help you speak your inner truth and enjoy serenity.

# OTHER AQUARIUS SUPPORT CRYSTALS

The following crystals are helpful for all Aquarius placements – your Sun, Moon, Rising Sign and any other Aquarius planet or point you may have in your chart. Harness the potential of these stones for clarity and ease in important life areas.

Everyone has different goals for romantic love. In addition, your wishes or desires can change over time. You may wish to attract or pursue love. Perhaps you are hoping to deepen your ability to love, or to open up to intimacy physically, emotionally or spiritually. Aquarius's relationships are enlightening and invigorating. When you feel inspired by the potential and unique qualities of a relationship, you thrive. This is especially true if a relationship offers you the freedom to be yourself. Love, for you, is often rooted in friendship. You are happy to fly solo, but, if the mood strikes you, you can be a loyal long-term partner. Choose a crystal ally that can support you in feeling secure and sharing your thoughts with clarity.

**JOY
SECURITY
COMMUNICATION**

**Ruby Fuchsite** Ruby Fuchsite energetically builds you up so that you feel confident, secure and ready for love. Aquarius is known to take it slow and keep it cool in relationships. Let Ruby Fuchsite ramp up your joy and bliss quotient, so you're less likely to hold back when it comes to expressing yourself. This naturally formed fusion of fire-red Ruby and mint-green Fuchsite combines passion with practicality. It's a perfect match for you, with your trademark blend of fun and restraint, and, as such, it can help you know what's true for you and help you communicate honestly in love.

Friends offer support, fun, love and new perspectives. With Aquarius prominently placed in your chart, you are a social honeybee, but you relish your freedom and alone time. You bring your friends the gifts of adventure, fun times, riveting conversation and teamwork. No one can dream bigger than you, and you inspire your friends to imagine new possibilities. In classic contradictory fashion, Aquarius brings people together, but often feels left out. You're supported by a crystal that helps you trust that you are included and accepted for who you are.

**Bismuth**   This crystalline metal brings people together. You are a natural connector and Bismuth helps you remember that you are also supported in your community, that you are loved and accepted. Bismuth is a native element that can grow beautiful, multi-coloured and iridescent crystals. This semi-metal is grounding and stabilizing – it helps you stand up for your unique self and follow your own path in life. It also reminds you to trust that you don't have to walk this path alone. Invite your friends to join you on your fantastic journey with the help of Bismuth!

**COMMUNITY**
**SECURITY**
**COMFORT**

Astrological insight can help galvanize your natural talents with your money-making potential. Your Aquarius prosperity gifts are philanthropy, imagination, genius, progress, uniqueness and community. If you'd like to make more money, look to these qualities for inspiration. What do you love to think about? How can you give back to society? Aquarius has contradictory money habits. To outsiders, your financial choices may seem erratic, but you have your reasons. By default, you are a bit miserly. This is because you think ten steps ahead, so your dreams and fears for the future have a big impact on your everyday habits. However, a few situations find you spending – trends, new technologies, philanthropy and exploring new horizons.

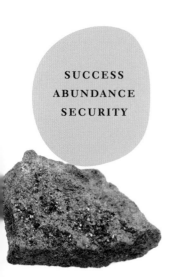

SUCCESS
ABUNDANCE
SECURITY

**Uvarovite Garnet**   The lush green hue of Uvarovite Garnet calls to mind verdant pine forests. Let this evergreen crystal vitalize your financial prospects and bring you abundant growth. Uvarovite Garnet is a silicate mineral that helps you grow deep roots so you feel steady and secure financially. From a place of stability, you can expand by investing in your dreams and visions. No crystal is a magic money potion, but this stone prompts you to believe in yourself and trust in your future, while simultaneously forming solid habits and making responsible decisions.

When leadership and vision are required, people turn to you. You honour the past, but you know exactly when it's time to disrupt tradition for the sake of a better future. This knack for progress, paired with your keen conceptual mindset, makes you a shoo-in for the leadership role. Or maybe you'd rather set out on your own because your unconventional spirit has no patience for pandering to the establishment. Either way, you get things done. Your keyword when it comes to work is 'innovation'. You can almost smell the next version, the future trend, the better way forwards. Work should be exciting, progressive and thought-provoking. The cutting edge is your comfort zone.

**Girasol Quartz**  An amplifying silicate crystal, Girasol Quartz helps you tune in to and magnify your dreams. With the help of this foggily translucent stone, set your sights on important work goals and focus your actions so that you can follow through. You are motivated when you feel that you are moving forwards, and you get frustrated when you're bored. Use this crystal to help you soften your approach, so that you can ease the frustration that may come with a realistic timeline.

You don't give up easily and, when you believe in something, you push for it. Girasol Quartz helps you set your focus and then work step-by-step to create the future of your dreams.

**FOCUS
ENHANCEMENT
CUSHIONING**

Your energy is lively and dynamic. You ponder the future and you're always a few steps ahead. Harness this aptitude to create long-term goals for a healthy lifestyle. If thoughts of the future are worrying, try calming meditative practices to soothe you and calm your mind. As an intellectual Air sign, you tend to focus on your thoughts and forget about your body. Creating a routine to support your basic health is therefore helpful. Technology excites you, so using fitness apps, trackers and wearable devices in your everyday life may be the support you need to meet your health goals. A hyper-personalized approach to your health suits you, and you may enjoy alternative or holistic healing practices.

**PRACTICALITY**
**RELAXATION**
**SUPPORT**

**Hematite**  Hematite can help you relax and be present in the moment. With this lustrous black crystal by your side, you may feel more centred in your body as it is a stone of grounding, balancing and protection. Hematite is an excellent aid for creating preventative health habits that stick. It helps you settle down and take a practical approach. Reach for Hematite when you need a gentle prodding to get back to basics and look out for your health and well-being.

# AQUARIUS THROUGHOUT THE YEAR

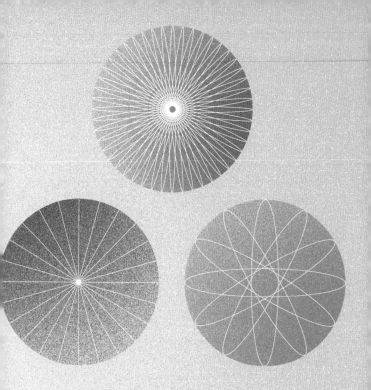

The energies of the zodiac signs affect us throughout the year. In astrology, there is a season for everything. Feeling separated from nature's cycles and rhythms can make you feel out of step or off-kilter. It may add to stress and drain energy. Understanding and attuning to astrology's seasons might help you feel enlivened.

Take this attunement one step further by using crystals to amplify the unique energy of each moment, so that you feel fully aligned with the rhythms of nature.

The following pages take you on a journey with the sun as it passes through the twelve signs of the zodiac on its annual rotation. You will discover the key energies of each season, along with a sign-specific horoscope that aligns with the important themes of your unique chart.

# CONFIDENCE AND LEADERSHIP

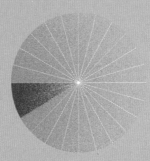

Aries season is the signal that begins the horse race.
And they're off! This is the moment to gallop at top speed
towards your goals. Put yourself out there with confidence.
Make bold decisions and step in time with your intuition.
This season is about saying YES to who you are and living
your life with freedom. The buds are beginning to emerge
and new life is beginning. Sync up with this feeling of
potential and possibility.

## AQUARIUS HOROSCOPE FOR ARIES SEASON

Enliven your mind with new ideas and realizations. The Sun is touring your zone of mental and social connections. You may feel filled with curiosity as you seek out learning opportunities. Your desire to communicate and share with others is also heightened. Get on the phone, crack open a book or chat with a neighbour. You never know what you may discover.

**Morning Practice**

Get your heart rate up with
some fiery cardio exercise.

**Evening Practice**

Cool down that inner
fire with a soothing herbal tea.

CRYSTALS FOR
ARIES SEASON

## CONFIDENCE

**Hessonite Garnet**    Developing confidence is a practice of
establishing deep self-trust. Let Hessonite Garnet's activating
and powerful energy help you build up your courage so that
you can just go for it. Also try Green Aventurine, Orange
Calcite or Malachite.

## LIVING BOLDLY

**Pink Aventurine**    When the time is ripe for taking bold
action, Pink Aventurine can help you advance into your next
adventure. Reach for it when you need a boost of fun. This
spirited crystal connects you with your heart centre, and acts
as your best accomplice in bravery and boldness. Or choose
Ruby, Tangerine Quartz or Sardonyx.

## DRIVE

**Fire Agate**    Aries season is the vehicle in which to follow
your passions and desires, which makes Fire Agate the
gasoline. Whether you need to get an important project
going or just tackle spring cleaning, put yourself on track to
get things done by syncing up with the vibration of this fierce
crystal. You could also reach for Bloodstone, Stromatolite
or Cinabrite.

# MONEY AND SELF-WORTH

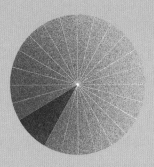

Like working in a garden and then enjoying the beauty that you've cultivated, Taurus represents sustained effort that leads to a productive reward. This season is the prime time to focus on building up your sense of personal worth and value. On one level, this process may involve nurturing your self-esteem. On another level, this may include thinking about security, money and finances. Taurus season is also a time to remember the beauty of life. It reminds us that no matter what is going on, there are simple pleasures to be had

## AQUARIUS HOROSCOPE FOR TAURUS SEASON

Slow down and retreat into the safety of your inner sanctum. The Sun is lighting up your sector of tender emotions, home and family. During this introspective season you may want to spruce up your home or connect with a long-lost family member. Or you may just want to spend this time alone letting your feelings and emotions flow as you reflect on the past.

| Morning Practice | Evening Practice |
|---|---|
| Practice gratitude by reminding yourself of three things you're grateful for. | Do something that feels good to your body, like stretching or wearing soft clothing. |

CRYSTALS FOR TAURUS SEASON

## MONEY MAGIC

**Green Jade**   No matter where you are beginning financially, Green Jade will juice up your money situation. This abundance stone has a way of amplifying your potential. A soft and expansive prosperity stone that soothes the spirit, it will support you as you make wise financial decisions. Reach for it when you crave a feeling of security. You could also use Pyrite, Emerald or Epidote.

## SELF-WORTH

**Red Jasper**   Red Jasper will amp up your self-appreciation quotient. Choose Red Jasper when you're feeling uncertain, if your confidence could use a boost, or if you want to feel more resilient in any way. This stone will get you in the groove of trusting your own value. Also try Carnelian, Chrysocolla or Bixbite.

## ABUNDANCE

**Green Apatite**   If you are feeling like something in your life is lacking, such as money, time, energy, sleep, or support, for example, you might need to boost your sense of abundance. Taurus season is the perfect time to grasp hold of that feeling of nature's plentifulness. Use Green Apatite to replenish your energy and help you feel satisfied and satiated with what you have. You could also reach for Golden Tourmaline, Uvarovite Garnet or Agate.

# VALUES
# AND COMMUNITY

Gemini energy is like a buzzing bee that moves from flower to flower in a garden. This season is a time of mental stimulation, new ideas, learning, communicating and sharing. Use Gemini season to evaluate or challenge your mindset and values. Which attitudes are no longer serving you? What's truly important to you? Gemini season is also a time to connect with others in the community. What can you learn from others? What can you teach others? It's a fun and lively season full of new connections.

## AQUARIUS HOROSCOPE
## FOR GEMINI SEASON

Turn up the volume on fun, sparkle and flair! During this glittery season you are called to be bold and be yourself. You have a lot to share with the world, so don't hold back. Other people are inspired by your unique individuality. If your hobbies and talents have been collecting dust, now is the time to revive your creative spirit and remember what brings you enjoyment.

**Morning Practice**

Help a new mindset emerge with a potent Gemini season intention.

**Evening Practice**

Before falling asleep, envision yourself having a great time at a party surrounded by everyone you love.

CRYSTALS FOR GEMINI SEASON

## MASTER YOUR MINDSET

**Heliodor**  Have repeating thoughts, fears or anxieties been plaguing you? Use the revitalizing energy of Gemini season and Heliodor to hit the reset button on these old thought patterns. This stone will gently help you harmonize your thoughts and adjust your mindset, helping you reconnect with your true values. Alternatively, try Blue Lace Agate, Chrome Chalcedony or Dragonstone.

## CONNECTING

**Agatized Coral**  When you really want to feel connected, seen, heard and understood, reach for Agatized Coral. This fossilized coral nudges you to reach out to others and helps you analyse your relationships, whether with friends, lovers, family, neighbours or colleagues. It relays an upbeat feeling so that you can view your relationships with the people in your life with optimism. You may also choose Citrine, Apricot Agate or Bismuth.

## COMMUNICATION

**Aquamarine**  Aquamarine is your crystal-clear communication companion. Communication helps us feel connected, and allows us to learn and grow. In those moments when you feel confused or foggy, this elegant stone will help you become grounded and steady. Use Aquamarine to find your voice – it will help you tune into your own true message and the truth of those around you. Alternatively, reach for Turquoise, Prairie Tanzanite or Green Chrysocolla.

# HOME AND NURTURE

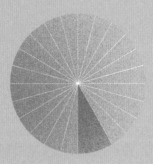

Come on home to Cancer season. Like Cancer's symbol, the Crab, wrap yourself in a protective shell and reflect on your life and your feelings. In Cancer season, engage in meaningful self-care, and also put your energy into nurturing others. Discover what makes you feel safe and cosy. This could be your actual home, your closest relationships or tending to the feelings and needs of your inner child.

## AQUARIUS HOROSCOPE FOR CANCER SEASON

Pay close attention to the details. The Sun is moving through your zone of organization, health and habits. Everything that has to do with the mundane aspects of daily life is up for review. What needs to be done to make things work more smoothly? You currently have the energy to make minor changes that can have a big impact.

I NURTURE MYSELF AND ACCEPT MYSELF
JUST AS I AM.

**Morning Practice**

Let your inner child take the lead:
what do they want to do today?

**Evening Practice**

Sing a lullaby to soothe your
inner child before bed.

CRYSTALS FOR
CANCER SEASON

## NURTURING

**Blue Calcite**   What do you want to actively care for?
Yourself? A child? A creative project? In order to feel truly
nurturing, you need to feel inspired by love. Blue Calcite will
help you soften and open up your heart centre, so that you
feel drawn to put your compassionate and attentive energy
where it is needed most. Other nurturing crystals include
Moonstone, Blue Chalcedony and Bumblebee Jasper.

## HOME ENVIRONMENT

**Pink Mangano Calcite**   Home is where you are safe and
protected. It's your emotional nest where you can relax. Use
Pink Mangano Calcite to create a grounded and peaceful
home environment. This stone acts as a balm that will help
you feel harmonized. Place this rosy crystal in your inner
sanctum and set the intention to soothe conflict and soften
your environment so that you can restore your energy after a
long day or week. You could also try Chiastolite, Rose Quartz
or Peach Moonstone.

## FAMILY BONDS

**Bornite**   Family, whether chosen or blood-related, represent
some of our closest relationships. Use Bornite to foster the
strength of family relationships. This is a joyful stone that
will help you embrace the positives that come from your
family circle, while at the same time grounding you to help
you remember who you are as an individual. Also try Orange
Calcite, Indigo Gabbro or Girasol Quartz.

# CREATIVITY AND FUN

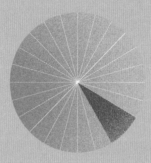

Harnessing your creativity and expressing your true self with others, that's the key to making the most of Leo season. It's all about playful sharing and creative shining. Radiate your magnificent heart of gold outwards with immediacy, freedom, spontaneity, generosity and a giant sense of fun. During this season of wholehearted self-expression, take a little time to remember how unique you are. Remember what inspires you and reflect on what you love most about yourself.

## AQUARIUS HOROSCOPE FOR LEO SEASON

Focus your attention on your important relationships. The Sun is moving through the zone of partnership, and that means it is shining a spotlight on the most important people in your life.

Are there words that have been left unspoken? Maybe boundaries that need to be set? Appreciation that you would like to convey? Communicate what's on your mind.

**Morning Practice**

Create daily.

**Evening Practice**

Seek out a chance to laugh every day and go to bed with a smile on your face.

## INSPIRATION

**Rutilated Quartz**  Inspiration is the creative spark and Rutilated Quartz can help you turn that spark into a roaring bonfire. Make Leo season feel lit up with creativity. Keep Rutilated Quartz by your side when you need an inventive solution to a problem at work, when your love life could use an inspiring reboot, or when you are ready to awaken the artist within. Set your intentions and let this highly programmable stone carry the flame of your dreams. You could also use Sunstone, Golden Labradorite or Yellow Sapphire.

## SELF-APPRECIATION

**Thulite**  Leo season is the time to shed all insecurities and put your faith in your one true self. Loving yourself dissolves insecurity and self-criticism. Thulite tunes you into the vibration of love, peace and harmony, allowing you to be present and wholly yourself. Alternatively, reach for Ruby, Larimar, or Desert Jasper.

## COURAGE

**Golden Apatite**  To ensure your lion-heartedness knows no bounds, you need to fire up your courage. Golden Apatite bestows upon you both passion and discernment, which determine which fears are baseless. Use it when you need to take a risk at work, strike up a conversation with someone you admire or stand up for your values. Other courage-giving crystals are Carnelian, Iolite-Sunstone or Citrine.

# HEALTH
# AND HABITS

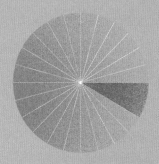

Our goals and dreams require a big-picture view,
but Virgo season reminds us that life is actually lived in the
small details. Focus on how you are living your life, your
everyday routines and rituals. On a practical level, what is
important to you? Virgo energy helps you take a closer
look at your health and habits, and how you can be
of service to others as well.

## AQUARIUS HOROSCOPE
## FOR VIRGO SEASON

The season is ripe for change and transformation. The Sun is lighting up your area of renewal. It's time to let go of the past, feel your feelings, forgive and release. This process makes room for new beginnings and emotional rebirth. During this tender time, let your emotions flow and be honest with yourself about what you're feeling.

| **Morning Practice** | **Evening Practice** |
|---|---|
| Drink a glass of water first thing. | Write down one task you're going to complete tomorrow, and stick to it. |

## FOCUS

**Clear Quartz**  Virgo season ushers in a chance to notice the details and get focused. Use Clear Quartz to take you all the way there. This cleansing stone helps you rivet your attention on your commitments. When you program Clear Quartz with your intention for focus, you'll find that it supports you, whether you have a tight deadline or you just really need to concentrate. You could also turn to Vanadinite, Amazonite or Tiger Iron.

## HEALTH

**Chevron Amethyst**  A lot of factors go into maintaining optimum health: genetics, diet, exercise, access to care, to name just a few. Virgo season energy will encourage you to think wisely about the preventative measures that you can take to boost both your mental well-being and physical health. Use Chevron Amethyst for gentle motivation that can help you happily embrace healthier choices. Or try Girasol Quartz, Ruby Fuchsite or Black Tourmaline.

## ALTRUISM

**Stromatolite**  Humanity wouldn't be a successful species without the desire to be of service to others. Virgo season plus Stromatolite is your recommendation for kindness and selfless action. Turn your attention to what you can do to help others, whether that's volunteering, making a donation to a good cause, or simply smiling and being friendly. Let Stromatolite amplify your altruistic nature. Alternatively, reach for Stichtite, Rhodonite or Rose Quartz.

# RELATIONSHIPS AND BALANCE

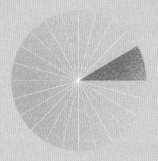

Libra season is symbolized by balanced scales.
It's a chance to look at all life areas and judge the
equilibrium. Are your relationships in balance? Do both
people in your relationships have what they want and
need? This can be a fun and harmonious time to socialize.
During Libra season, balance can also be created in your
environment through art, decoration and organization.
The scales are the symbol for justice and Libra season brings
a collective yearning to make the systems of government
more fair and to expose inequalities.

## AQUARIUS HOROSCOPE FOR LIBRA SEASON

Adventure is beckoning. The world
is vast and there is much to learn.
The Sun is traversing your sector of
expansion and philosophy. You can
explore through travel, as you see new
things and discover different ways to
live. Or you can open a good book
and learn about life from the comfort
of home. Either way, prepare to open
your mind.

## Affirmation

### BALANCE EXISTS IN
### ALL AREAS OF MY LIFE.

**Morning Practice**

Reach out and message
someone who is important to
you, and tell them why.

**Evening Practice**

Meditate to create
mental balance.

## HEALTHY BOUNDARIES

**Iolite**   Communicating what you want, need and desire is a
great starting point to gain clarity in your relationships. Iolite
can help you reflect and get to know yourself – the first step to
speaking and sharing your truth with others. Once your inner
base is stabilized, Iolite can help you reach out to another
person, while maintaining your own healthy boundaries. This
healing stone has a peaceful energy that helps you create
balance between yourself and a partner. You could also use
Amazonite, Purple Jade or Chiastolite.

## BALANCE

**Shungite**   Balance is an active state, requiring constant
adjustment. It comes under the jurisdiction of the intellectual,
analytical sign of Libra. Keep checking in with yourself
throughout Libra season to determine what needs more
balance. For a crystal that will help you stay steady, reach for
Shungite. Or choose Diopside, Selenite or Turquoise.

## DECISIVENESS

**Ametrine**   Libra season is an excellent time to analyse, think
things through and come up with new ideas. Keep Ametrine
by your desk for productive planning sessions and for when you
have big decisions to make. This balancing stone will help you
keep your life on track. As an alternative, try Variscite, Fluorite
or White Sapphire.

# TRANSFORMATION AND FORGIVENESS

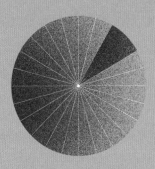

Scorpio season pulls you deeper – emotionally, physically and spiritually. This is a season of transformation, helping you to feel deeply, release old emotions and thought patterns, and get ready to move on to the next stage. By pulling back the layers and being honest with the truth of who you are, it's also an opportunity to deepen your relationships with others by letting them get to know the real you.

## AQUARIUS HOROSCOPE FOR SCORPIO SEASON

The Sun is lighting up your work zone. Career and vocation are asking for your attention. You'll be making big moves, keeping busy or finding a new direction. If there was ever a time for action, this would be it. Be strategic though, and make sure that your energy is being used productively. Now is the moment to make some solid plans and prioritize your ambitions.

| **Morning Practice** | **Evening Practice** |
| --- | --- |
| Forgive yourself for something. | Forgive someone else for something. |

**CRYSTALS FOR SCORPIO SEASON**

## INTIMACY

**Red Tourmaline**   Scorpio season propels you to create warmth and closeness. But opening yourself up to the vulnerability of intimacy demands courage. Whether you are setting the stage for sexual intimacy or emotional intimacy, Red Tourmaline will help you feel confident enough to embrace deep connection with others. Other crystals for intimacy are Garnet, Shiva Lingam or Red Aventurine.

## TRANSFORMATION

**Moldavite**   Transformation brings both endings and new beginnings. Moldavite will help you spiritually and emotionally adjust when change comes into your life – when a relationship has run its course, a shift is needed in the work arena or a new adventure calls your name. When the transformation you are undergoing is more subtle in texture, like saying goodbye to an old habit, Moldavite will help you align with your new reality. Or try Shungite, Moss Agate or Tugtupite.

## FORGIVENESS

**Dioptase**   Whether you need to be kinder to yourself or let go of hurt that someone else has caused you, forgiveness doesn't happen all at once. It's a process that you set in motion. Finding forgiveness requires self-love, self-worth and understanding. Dioptase can help you practice forgiveness by supporting you with its gentle and loving vibrations. You could also turn to Black Moonstone, Rhodochrosite or Pink Tourmaline.

# WISDOM
# AND FREEDOM

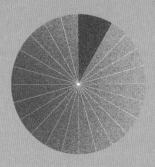

Sagittarius season is represented by the archer who shoots high and blazes a trail into new territory. The archer is also a centaur – half horse and half human, half wild and half philosophical. Sagittarius season is a time to feel fiercely alive and simultaneously inspired to ask big, existential questions. It's a season for expanding your boundaries and traveling physically and mentally to understand more about the world and the human experience.

## AQUARIUS HOROSCOPE
## FOR SAGITTARIUS SEASON

Invigorate your hopes and dreams. As always, the sky is the limit, so don't think about what's probable, instead entice your imagination by mulling over everything that's possible. Your naturally innovative nature can really shine right now, as the Sun puts a spotlight on your aspirations and visions for the future.

| **Morning Practice** | **Evening Practice** |
| --- | --- |
| Go for a walk or a jog out in nature. | Memorize an inspiring quote. |

CRYSTALS FOR SAGITTARIUS SEASON

### INNER WISDOM

**Azurite**   In Sagittarius season, the archer knows that the best way to take aim is to trust your inner wisdom. When you are connected to your true self, it's easier to make choices. Life feels more satisfying. Azurite is the stone to hold and carry when you want to bolster your self-confidence and tune into your wisdom. Or choose Idocrase, Shattuckite or Amethyst.

### EXPANSION

**Jasper**   Ruled by the gas giant Jupiter, Sagittarius is the sign of expansion. During this season, you can move beyond anything that is limiting you. Is there an area of your life in which you feel trapped in a cage? Maybe if you take a closer look, you'll find that the door to the cage has been open the entire time. Feel the freedom and expansion that is available to you with the help of Jasper. This enlivening stone will help you break out into new territory. Alternatives are Blue Topaz, Pink Chalcedony or Ruby Iolite.

### ADVENTURE AND TRAVEL

**Turquoise**   When you're setting out in search of new horizons, reach for Turquoise as your talisman for protection and luck. Travel and adventure require equal parts bravery and boldness, but the reward is an expanded mindset and perspective. Let Turquoise be your steady support system as you push beyond your boundaries to discover excitement, new opportunity and enlightenment. You could also use Green Opal, Smoky Quartz or Aventurine.

# CAREER
# AND GOALS

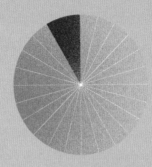

Like the mountain goat, in Capricorn season
you are primed to choose your footing carefully as
you make your ascent. Capricorn season brings practical
and productive forward motion. Use this energy efficiently
and tactically. You may choose to counterbalance this drive
and ambition with a large dose of acceptance, both
of yourself and others. Remember to give yourself a
break; you are trying your best.

## AQUARIUS HOROSCOPE
## FOR CAPRICORN SEASON

Remove distractions and unplug.
For Aquarius, this is a wonderful
opportunity to take a break and restore
your energy. Next month brings an
extraverted season, so prepare for
that by checking in with your inner
world. What are you feeling? How
can you soothe yourself? Do you need
more rest? Unstructured time can be
restorative. Let yourself drift and dream

**Morning Practice**

Write down your goals.

**Evening Practice**

Reflect on your
accomplishments.

CRYSTALS FOR
CAPRICORN SEASON

## ACHIEVEMENT

**Fluorite**   Your Capricorn season recommendation supports
you in taking things one step at a time while staying focused
on your big picture goals. Look to Fluorite. Fluorite's unique
vibration can help you concentrate, while energizing you so
that you can keep moving forwards. Or look for support from
Ocean Jasper, Septarian Nodule or Tiger's Eye.

## CAREER

**Cat's Eye**   Capricorn season is a wonderful time to take
stock. While you think about your work life, keep Cat's Eye by
your side. This stone helps you know your strengths, which is
imperative for a fulfilling career. It will help you feel optimistic
and believe in yourself. Cat's Eye's structured energy helps
you know your personal boundaries and make smart money
choices. You could also use Andradite Garnet, Apatite or
Hawk's Eye.

## FOR SELF-ACCEPTANCE

**Blue Aragonite**   Let calming Blue Aragonite guide you
when you need to feel the soothing balm of self-acceptance.
Capricorn season pushes you to achieve, which may cause
you to question your progress in life. Counterbalance that by
learning to accept yourself for who you are. Blue Aragonite
has a compassionate energy that may inspire you to be less
judgemental towards yourself and show yourself more kindness.
Other crystals for self-acceptance are Prasiolite, Amethyst
or Shungite.

# FRIENDSHIP AND VISION

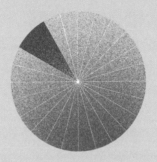

Aquarius season pushes people and ideas to the forefront. What are your big ideas for the future? And who is in your community? Your vision for the future may also be a vision for humanity. Take the time to research causes to which you might contribute time, money and resources. Your friends, communities and social groups are extra important during this season, so prioritize the people who mean the most to you.

## AQUARIUS HOROSCOPE FOR AQUARIUS SEASON

This is your special season! With the Sun touring your zone of personality and identity, you can sparkle – it's time to show the world exactly who you are! Be spontaneous and free. Do the activities that fill you with joy! Maybe it's time to change your look or test out a new hobby. Don't be afraid to be a little bit weird, that's part of your Aquarius special sauce. You are unique and radiant.

**Morning Practice**

Create a vision board and make it the
first thing you see when you wake up.

**Evening Practice**

Call a friend for a
meaningful chat.

### FRIENDSHIP

**Bismuth**   Aquarius season asks you to turn towards your
community. What can you offer? What will you receive?
Friends enrich your life in so many ways, but mostly by
encouraging your feeling of belonging – a natural mood
booster. Bismuth has an expansive energy that helps you join
with others in a shared sense of community. Carry Bismuth as a
reminder that you are connected to others. Or you could reach
for Carnelian, Sunset Sodalite or Blue Apatite.

### FAITH IN THE FUTURE

**Cavansite**   The future is uncertain. Sometimes you need a
boost to help you trust in the potential and possibility of what
the future can become. In that case, reach for Cavansite.
This stone has a sweet vibe of positivity that can give you the
courage to believe in your biggest dreams for the future. Some
alternatives are Peridot, Muscovite or Auralite 23.

### VIBRATIONAL LIFT

**Apophyllite**   When Aquarius season asks you to turn
your attention to what is possible, it helps to have a positive
outlook. Without suppressing any challenging feelings (those
are important and need to be processed), pay some special
attention to the positive things in your life and work to create
an enduring, positive mindset. If you need a little extra support,
reach for Clear or Green Apophyllite. This high-vibe crystal
can lift your spirits and help you feel full of potential. You
could also try Quartz, Hematite or Angelite.

# INTUITION AND SPIRITUALITY

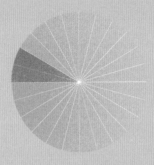

The most mystical season of all, Pisces season is the time to tune into your intuition. Slide like a slippery fish into the sphere of your dreams, faith, spirituality, compassion and creativity. This is a moment to rest, reflect and look inwards. Reconnect with your imagination. Feel your feelings. Plug into your spirituality or whatever makes you feel connected to the universe.

## AQUARIUS HOROSCOPE FOR PISCES SEASON

Even though the Sun is moving through the dreamy sign of Pisces, Aquarius people will feel inspired to find stable footing on solid ground. The Sun is traversing your zone of money, resources and self-worth. Evaluate your financial priorities. Discover what security means to you. Use this season to expand your trust in yourself, so that you feel thoroughly confident and capable.

**Morning Practice**

Record your dreams.

**Evening Practice**

Do some freewriting
to clear your mind.

CRYSTALS FOR
PISCES SEASON

## COMPASSION

**Lavender Quartz**  Lavender Quartz helps you feel peace and
understanding for others. It will bestow upon you the softness
that you need to open up to other people's perspectives. It will
also allow you to dissolve drama with a heightened sense of
empathy. This soothing and healing stone can offer strength
while you stand in someone else's shoes. A compassionate life
is a fulfilling life. As an alternative, turn to Thulite, Prehnite
with Epidote or Fluorite.

## INTUITION

**Pink Opal**  When you trust your inner guidance system you
have ultimate clarity. Harness the power of your intuition
in Pisces season with the help of Pink Opal. This stone will
help you connect to yourself and to your guides. It raises
the volume on your inner 'Yes' or 'No' by quietening any
distractions and helping you connect within. Other crystals
for intuition are Clear Quartz, Moldavite or Dumortierite.

## FOR FAITH

**Celestite**  Faith can be thought of as a complete trust or
confidence in someone or something. With a little bit of
faith you may find it easier to contend with fear or anxiety.
But trust and faith must be developed from within. In Pisces
season, harness the power of high-vibrational Celestite to
help you move beyond unnecessary fears as you put your
trust in something bigger. You could also use Vatican Stone,
Apophyllite or Turquoise.

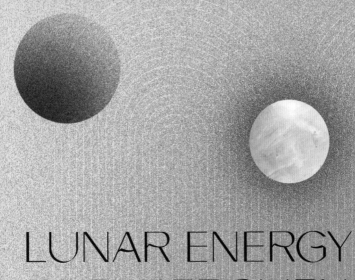

# LUNAR ENERGY
# AND MERCURY
# IN MOTION

# THE LUNAR
# CYCLE

In astrology, the Moon is a catalyst, helping us to move forwards with our goals and intentions.

The 29-day lunar cycle begins in darkness. The Moon then appears as a faint crescent and grows bigger until it's full. This process, from darkness to Full Moon, mirrors the incubation and development of your own creative process. Then, the Moon wanes until it completely disappears, reflecting another stage of the creative cycle – the process of releasing your efforts and making space for another cycle to begin. This allows new thoughts and ideas to emerge.

Each of the eight phases of the Moon cycle offers a different type of energy, which we will explore in this chapter. You can follow the Moon through the lunar month with crystal recommendations, setting your intentions in alignment with the New Moon and letting the lunar cycle help you make that intention into reality. The lunar cycle will also help you cleanse and release so that you can gently transition into the next phase.

By using crystals to work with the lunar cycle you can activate the potential of the Moon and amplify its energy. Through visualization or meditation, tap into the unique energies of each stage of the Moon cycle with the following crystals. For the suggested rituals at each phase, choose a crystal from the recommended options, or substitute with your favourite crystal.

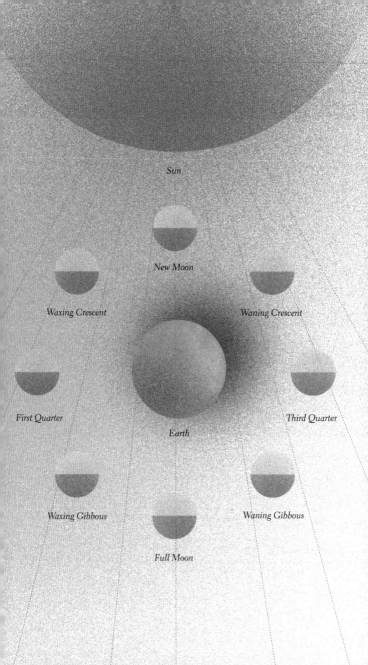

Sun

New Moon

Waxing Crescent

Waning Crescent

Waxing Gibbous

Full Moon

Waning Gibbous

First Quarter

Third Quarter

Earth

## SET YOUR NEW INTENTIONS

The Moon is dark. This is a time for reflection and a time to connect with your inner self. Use your energy to envision what you would like to make happen. What do you desire? What are your dreams? Anything is possible – imagine that you are planting seeds of intention that will manifest and grow throughout the Waxing Moon Phase. The New Moon is a quiet and emotional time and you may discover that, as you think about what you would like to create, many different feelings arise. Excitement, anticipation, fear, worry – whatever feelings arise, make space for those feelings and be gentle with yourself. Listen to your intuition and imagine your next steps.

**Black Moonstone** can support you during the delicate and sensitive New Moon vibration. It offers wellsprings of patience and peace as you work with your emotions and reflect on your life. When your dreams are germinating under the surface, Black Moonstone can help you trust your own process.

**Labradorite** opens your third eye wide so that you can tune into your intuition, and design your goals in accordance with your path and purpose.

**Pink Sapphire's** loving energy can buffer you and help you feel emotionally at ease.

**Ametrine** provides sweet joy and concentrated focus so that you can set intentions with confidence.

TRUST,
INSPIRATION, SERENITY
AND DELIGHT

### New Moon Ritual

Freewrite about what you yearn for and anything else that's on your mind. Then jot down your intentions for this Moon cycle on a piece of paper and place your chosen crystal on top.

# NURTURE YOUR INTENTIONS

Your seeds of intention are germinating under the soil, and maybe some of the plants are just beginning to sprout. As the lunar energy builds momentum, make sure that you have the resources you need to achieve your goals. Provide structure and support for yourself. This cycle is just beginning to take shape, so consider how your choices will determine your direction – maybe there are changes you'd like to make to your goals. Remain curious throughout this process, because anything is possible!

**Turquoise** is a powerhouse of a crystal that can deftly carry you through the precarious Waxing Crescent phase. At this moment you need a subtle combination of confidence, discernment, curiosity and commitment. Turquoise can help you understand the truth of what you need to create, and it can help you stay open and accepting of your process. Use this stone as you decide what you really want to manifest and commit to during this Moon cycle.

**Shattuckite** helps you intuitively illuminate your path so that you can make the decisions that are right for you.

**Pyrite** offers crystalline protection and is a wonderful choice to help you realize your goals.

**Orange Calcite** gives you mental focus and lots of energy for the journey ahead.

## TRUTH, INTUITION, MANIFESTATION AND FOCUS

### Waxing Crescent Moon Ritual

Read and rewrite your intentions for this Moon cycle.
Decorate the paper and place your chosen crystal back on top.

# BUILD YOUR MOMENTUM

Look around your garden of intentions and discover what is growing. Have your goals started to take shape? If so, how are they coming along? Do you need more support? Perhaps you have had surprising results? At the First Quarter Moon the constraints of reality can be intimidating. You have big dreams, but sometimes you encounter resistance when dreams make contact with real world limitations. Maybe there is more work required than you had foreseen, or there are real-world issues with time, money, support or other resources. Give yourself lots of encouragement. Pivot, and reassess if necessary. This is an exciting, high energy time, so keep taking action and building momentum.

**Bumblebee Jasper** When reality, and all of its limitations, hits, Bumblebee Jasper can help you stay the course with confidence. Lean on this crystal when you need the energy to just keep moving forwards. It will subdue your fears and inspire you to push past your comfort zone.

**Peridot** is a cheery companion that will help you look at any situation with optimism.

**Tangerine Quartz** offers creative potential that makes problem solving effortless.

**Aventurine** will vitalize you and give you the confidence to keep going.

CONFIDENCE,
OPTIMISM, CREATIVITY AND
VITALITY

**First Quarter Moon Ritual**

Light a candle, hold your chosen crystal and
visualize your intentions being realized.

# DEVELOP YOUR INTENTIONS

It's astonishing what a little effort can create! Now that you've made it to the Waxing Gibbous phase of the Moon cycle, you are starting to see the effects of the intentions that you set. If your goal was to improve your nutrition, you may be feeling better already. If you felt motivated to get out there and start dating, you may have started some new conversations. Whatever the last few days have revealed, now is the time to roll up your sleeves and actively give shape to your garden. What will you weed out? What is working, and what isn't working? What changes might you make? The intensity has almost peaked so take tender care of your emotional well-being as you keep putting in effort towards your dreams.

**Jet** Jet's grounding energy will help you establish deep root systems for your developing intentions. When you need strength and motivation to keep pushing forwards with your goals, this stone will support you. As a bonus, jet has a sheltering vibration that can steady you emotionally and help you surge forwards with optimism and hope.

**Hematite** offers balance and protection, helping you proactively take care of yourself during this active time.

**Carnelian** lights your fire with sparkling enthusiasm and convinces you to tune into your creative side.

**Blue Lace Agate** calms your mind, allowing you to weed through your options and make solid decisions.

### GROUNDING, PROTECTION, ENTHUSIASM AND PEACE OF MIND

---

### Waxing Gibbous Moon Ritual

While holding or wearing your chosen crystal, do something that feels active or expressive, such as dancing, painting, gardening, cooking or singing. Imagine your goals and repeat your intentions.

Everything is revealed under the light of the Moon. The attempts you've made, your wins, your losses. It's time to get out in the garden and harvest the crop. Regardless of whether the bounty lives up to your expectations, there is something to appreciate and celebrate. At the Full Moon, honour what you've created and give gratitude to yourself for your commitment. This phase represents the push and pull of two opposite energies as the Moon is in the opposite sign to the Sun. The result is a highly polarized and intense energy that can heighten emotions, pull you in two different directions, or cause you to realize something important. Make sure to be very gentle with yourself and those around you.

**EMOTIONAL EXPLORATION, ABUNDANCE, PEACEFULNESS AND RECEPTIVITY**

**White Moonstone** symbolizes the Full Moon and all of its glorious creativity and excitement. This pearly white crystal shines a bright light so that you can see clearly. As you examine the fruits that you've cultivated during the Waxing Moon phase, use the receptive and healing energy of White Moonstone to help you accept and celebrate. It's time for gratitude, and this comforting crystal will help you open up to that feeling.

**Green Apatite** is an antidote to the drama of the Full Moon – use it to highlight joy and abundance.

**Jade** has a subtle, soothing energy that imparts an optimistic attitude.

**Stilbite** connects the heart, mind and intuition – this can help you rationally balance your emotions while still opening up to divine insight.

**Full Moon Ritual**

Hold your chosen crystal and write down three things that you are grateful for. The Full Moon is also a great time to cleanse your crystals. Place them outside or on a windowsill and let them bathe in the Moon's healing energy.

# REFLECT AND REVIEW

Now that the intensity of the full reveal has begun to wane, you can settle deeper into your new reality. Indulge yourself and enjoy. As the Moon has moved through waxing to waning, this is the beginning of a less active and more receptive phase. This means that you can simply sit with the ebbing fullness of what is. Begin a process of compassionate review. What have you learned? What will you do differently in the next Moon cycle? Each lunar cycle reveals an older, more experienced version of who you are becoming. So sink into this moment of reflection and get to know yourself once more.

**Obsidian** offers a protective energy that buffers and supports. Use it at the Waning Gibbous phase of the Moon cycle to release the past and securely recline into the experience of the moment. Obsidian's cleansing vibes can help you remove any junk from your thought patterns, allowing you to think from a new perspective. Harness its clarifying energy to appraise your situation with equanimity and objectivity.

**Tiger's Eye** is for encouragement and strength as you review your progress and make plans for improvement.

**Citrine** offers joy and optimism so that you can look at your accomplishments through a positive lens.

**Celestite** provides tranquillity as you come down off the high of the Full Moon.

PROTECTION,
STRENGTH, JOY AND
TRANQUILLITY

### Waning Gibbous Moon Ritual

Pour yourself some tea, water, or other drink of your choice, and take the time to sit and quietly appreciate the moment. With your chosen crystal nearby, review your intention and gratitude lists.

# LET GO

Get comfortable letting go so that you can make space for new things. At the Last Quarter Moon allow the leaves to fall and the fading plants to return to the soil. A tree drops its leaves to conserve resources. Take stock of what you want to let go of, so that you can use your energy wisely. Is there someone you need to forgive? Do you need to release your expectations and accept something about your life? Release the past or an outdated way of thinking, let go and forgive. Maybe you declutter your closet, acknowledge your reality, admit your mistakes, get really honest with yourself, or forgive yourself or others. The Last Quarter Moon asks that you put in a little effort to let go of the emotions and ideas that are taking up excess energy.

## LOVE, SUPPORT, GROUNDING AND GENTLE SELF-REFLECTION

**Rose Quartz** is an emotional balm that can help you forgive yourself and others. As the Last Quarter Moon inspires you to release your expectations and accept your current reality, you need a soothing support that helps you open up compassionately. Rose Quartz brings playful, loving vibes and helps you gently accept a situation and move forwards.

**Rutilated Quartz** offers a powerful support in following through on your intentions as you review what you've learned and plan for the next phase.

**Smoky Quartz** provides grounding, protection and assistance in clearing the thoughts and feelings that you are ready to release.

**Amethyst** is for gently releasing old mental patterns and contemplating new possibilities.

---

### Last Quarter Moon Ritual

Create a peaceful environment and run a bath for yourself. Place a water-safe, non-toxic crystal (such as Quartz or Amethyst) in the bath while you review your intentions from this moon cycle. Repeat these affirmations, 'I make space for clarity' and 'I release the past'.

## STILLNESS AND REST

The lunar energy is encouraging you to turn inwards and be still. All is quiet in the winter of your metaphorical garden. Embracing stillness offers many benefits. By allowing your inner landscape to exist without judgement, you honour who you are now. Slowing down can also help you uncover your values and emotional truth – which may not be so apparent when you are busily running around. And last but not least, rest and quiet will help you recharge your energy for the next cycle. Challenge yourself to slow down and be present in the moment. There will be ample time for new plans and dreams when the next cycle begins.

**Serpentine** can help you open a gateway to the stillness within and to the profound interconnectedness of the universe. Using this crystal during your Waning Crescent Moon meditations will help you feel buffered and supported in the understanding that there is no-one you need to be and nothing you need to do. Float along with the waves of existence. You'll know when the time is right again for action.

**Selenite** radiates cleansing energy that can help you release the past cycle and prepare to make a fresh start.

**Howlite** soothes your spirit and quietens any absurd complaints from your 'inner critic'.

**Aquamarine** helps you create a meditative state of mind so that you can listen to the stillness within.

### CONNECTION WITH NATURE, CLEANSING, SOOTHING AND REFLECTION

---

### Waning Crescent Moon Ritual

Sit quietly in the meditation of your choosing. Hold your crystal or place it nearby.

# MERCURY RETROGRADE

Mercury Retrograde deserves attention as it's a chance to review your plans and goals. It's notoriously known for causing technology and communication issues, but the upside of this time period is that it offers an invitation to slow down and re-assess where you are and where you want to go.

Fast-moving Mercury symbolizes connection, communication and technology. Mercury is the part of you that learns, thinks, teaches and talks.

Mercury orbits the Sun about four times as fast as the Earth and every time that Mercury zips past the Earth an optical illusion occurs that makes it look as though Mercury is moving backwards. When Mercury appears to be moving backwards (Mercury Retrograde), it's a great opportunity to slow down. Go back over your thoughts and decisions of recent months and review them. Turn inwards to gain guidance from your intuition.

Mercury Retrograde happens about three times a year and lasts for about three weeks each time. You can use these retrograde periods as a moment to check in with yourself and review your practices, thoughts and relationships. Have you been putting off an uncomfortable conversation? Is there something that you need to be honest about with yourself when it comes to relationships, work or money? What has your body been trying to tell you? Is there some new way that you could step out of your comfort zone? What would help you feel more secure and supported?

Underlying issues tend to rise to the surface during Mercury Retrograde. It's typically advised to make sure that you are extra clear in your communications during these periods, and that you wait until the retrograde period has ended before beginning new projects or signing contracts. But it's an excellent time to pick up where you left off on something – to rethink, redo and review.

# YOUR CRYSTAL PRACTICE DURING MERCURY RETROGRADE

Crystal energy can help you slow down your busy mind and tune into your intuition during Mercury Retrograde. As you rethink and review, these crystals will amplify your intuition and clarity.

## KEEN INSIGHT

**Pietersite**  Employ this speckled Quartz for illuminated insight paired with steady determination.

## CLARITY AND COMMUNICATION

**Aquamarine**  This stone soothes and calms the mind while simultaneously boosting your ability to communicate clearly.

## CREATIVE THOUGHT

**Citrine**  A crystal that spurs your imagination, helping you conceptualize how you might like patterns or situations to change.

## Beginning of Mercury Retrograde Ritual

Perform a full and gentle review of the issues most affecting you by writing a journal entry using the following prompt: 'What do I need to see that I'm not seeing when it comes to my …' Give yourself lots of gratitude in the process and call on your chosen crystal to provide understanding and clarity. When you've finished, write down three takeaways on a small piece of paper and place your crystal on top of it for the remainder of the Retrograde. Drawing on the power of your crystal, let your subconscious mind continue to explore and reveal the subtleties of these thoughts and questions over the coming weeks.

## End of Mercury Retrograde Ritual

Near the end of the Retrograde cycle, set an intention to integrate what you've learned during the past days and weeks. Begin by returning to your piece of paper and your crystal. What came up for you during Mercury Retrograde? Was there a new realization, attitude or interest that emerged? Think about what you may have realized and journal about what you'd like to bring into your life now. Is there an intention (see page 22) or affirmation that could come from this exploration? If so, write it down. Look in a mirror and repeat your intention or affirmation five times while holding your crystal. Remember to thank your crystal and to thank yourself for showing up. For the next two weeks, repeat this daily ritual.

# CONCLUSION

---

This book has taken you deep below the Earth's surface, through the metaphorical caverns of crystals and their symbolism. You've connected the dots of the solar system and the meaning of the astrology you were born with. By pairing the forces of the stars above with the crystals below, you've gained tools that can help you navigate your unique journey with wisdom.

In Part Two, you learned about the crystals that can support your unique astrology. This section included insights for Aquarius Sun, Moon and Rising signs, along with supportive crystal recommendations for what your sign needs in five key life areas.

Life is always changing and so in Part Three you learned to follow the energy of the Sun as it moves on its annual journey through the zodiac, finding crystals that may help you elaborate on the theme of each astrological season.

Revolving and evolving with changing astrological cycles continued in Part Four, where you paired crystal energy with the ebb and flow of the Moon, and learned to harness the power of crystals in tandem with Mercury Retrograde to perform a trimonthly check-in.

All the answers are already within you. When you choose a crystal, you awaken the vibration of that crystal within yourself. Harness your astro-crystal practice to help you see what already exists inside of you. You have everything you need.

With the cosmos above and the crystals below, you are always connected and supported. Let the stones and the stars strengthen your self-awareness and self-trust as you continue your crystalline cosmic journey.

---

*Crystals and astrology are not intended to be a substitute for medical advice, diagnosis or treatment. Always seek the advice of your qualified healthcare provider.*

# RESOURCES

---

| | |
|---|---|
| GET YOUR BIRTH CHART | www.sandysitron.com/crystals |
| ASTROLOGY READING | www.sandysitron.com |
| CRYSTALS | *101 Power Crystals: The Ultimate Guide to Magical Crystals, Gems, and Stones for Healing and Transformation*<br>Judy Hall |
| CRYSTAL ENERGY HEALING | https://www.kalisaaugustine.com/ |
| SOURCING CRYSTALS RESPONSIBLY | moonrisecrystals.com/ |
| SPIRAL CRYSTALS | spiralcrystals.com/ |
| HOOF AND PAW | hoofandpawuk.com/ |
| ASTROLOGY | *Astrology for Yourself*<br>Demetra George and Douglas Bloch |
| AFFIRMATION WORK | Transformational coach Dana Balicki: https://danabalicki.com/ |
| AFFIRMATION WORK | *Empowerment: The Art of Creating Your Life as You Want It*<br>Gail Straub and David Gershon |
| ASTROLOGY EDUCATION | www.thestrology.com |
| | *Ritual Enchantments*<br>A Modern Witch's Guide to Self-Possession<br>Mya Spalter |

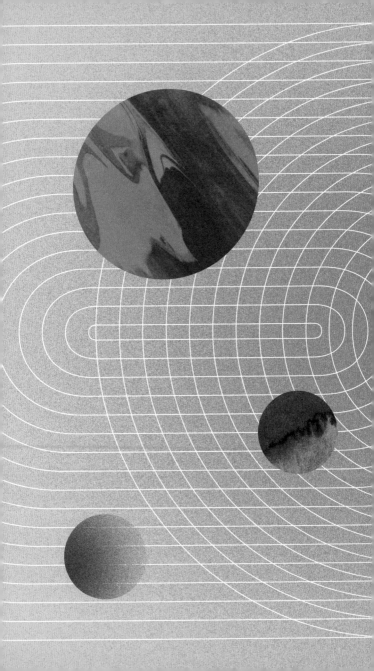

# FEATURED CRYSTALS

———

LAURENCE KING

First published in Great Britain in 2022 by Laurence King
an imprint of The Orion Publishing Group Ltd
Carmelite House, 50 Victoria Embankment
London EC4Y 0DZ

An Hachette UK Company

10 9 8 7 6 5 4 3 2 1

A CIP catalogue record for this book is
available from the British Library.

ISBN 978-0-8578-2923-8

Design: Therese Vandling

Printed in China by C&C Offset Printing Co. Ltd

Laurence King Publishing is committed to ethical and
sustainable production. We are proud participants in the
Book Chain Project®. [bookchainproject.com]

BOOK
CHAIN
PROJECT

www.laurenceking.com
www.orionbooks.co.uk